Decorating
with
Mosaics

Decorating
with
Mosaics

Deborah Schneebeli-Morrell

Over 20 step-by-step projects using
ceramics, glass, terracotta and pebbles

COLLINS & BROWN

For Deirdre Moylan, who helped me
piece together all the bits

First published in Great Britain in 1999
by Collins & Brown Limited
London House
Great Eastern Wharf
Parkgate Road
London SW11 4NQ

1 3 5 7 9 8 6 4 2

British Library Cataloguing-in-Publication Data:
A catalogue record for this book
is available from the British Library.

ISBN 1 85585 721 9

Editor: Gillian Haslam
Designer: Roger Daniels
Photographer: Heini Schneebeli
Stylist: Deborah Schneebeli-Morrell

Reproduction in Singapore
Printed and bound in China by Sun Fung

Author's Acknowledgements
Very special thanks to Heini Schneebeli for his care and attention to
detail in taking the lovely photographs in this book. As usual, my
friends have given me gifts of broken china at just the right time and
lent their beautiful homes and gardens for us to photograph in. They
are Raynes and Patrick Minns, Anna Bentinck and Arnold Cragg,
Jill Patchett and Alan Du Monceau, Sophie and Hugh Blackwell. A
special thank you to my unfailing and brilliant editor Gillian Haslam
and to Kate Kirby at Collins and Brown for her continuous and
optimistic support. My gratitude extends to all the unknown artists
and artisans whose work, particularly the exquisite painting on
antique ceramics, constantly serves as an inspiration to me.

Contents

Introduction

The history of the art of mosaics is a long and noble one. It is closely linked with decoration and function – key elements that have worked in conjunction with each other from the earliest times. In Ancient Greece the first pavements were made by assembling quantities of uncut coloured pebbles into decorative patterns, making a hard-wearing surface and giving structure to early urban development.

Right *Carefully cut patterned china has been used to create this colourful butterfly tile.*

Opposite *Paving slabs made from pebbles and terracotta make a stunning floor.*

Below *For a really dazzling effect, line a small bowl with random shards of silver porcelain.*

The Romans continued the craft, developing and refining the techniques by using naturally coloured marble and stone which they expertly cut into small tiles or tesserae. As well as patterns, intricate pictorial images were created using these small purpose-cut elements. Images from nature such as plants, birds, fish and animals were common themes for mosaics, as well as stylized depictions of the sacred world of the Gods. The invention of mortar, to be used between the tesserae as a form of grout, meant that these mosaics could be completely smooth and flat. As the influence of the Roman Empire spread to its furthest reaches, so did its crafts and traditions. The durability of mosaic work means that the legacy of the Ancient Romans can still be seen all over Europe.

The early Christian period brought with it a renewed interest in mosaic work. The exquisite Byzantine mosaics, most notably those at Ravenna in Italy, are made from glass smalti and use leaves of real gold sandwiched between the glass. The religious images were glorified and the richness of the Church was evident with the use of such valuable materials. Some people believe the distinction and quality of Byzantine mosaics has never been surpassed.

But the rich tradition of mosaic work has continued throughout the centuries, sometimes declining in popularity and at

other times being subject to a fashionable revival. The interest in arts and crafts at the turn of the nineteenth century meant that mosaic images became freer from their original connections with the Church and rich patronage. Through the influence of the Art Nouveau movement, artists introduced mosaics into everyday architecture such as shops and apartment buildings.

The inspirational and unique architecture of Spanish architect Antonio Gaudi in Barcelona, dating from the early twentieth century, exploits the use of mosaic on extravagant three-dimensional surfaces and has perhaps done more than others to inspire the current interest in mosaics. Throughout the twentieth century this trend has continued – mosaics now adorn everything from swimming pools to municipal buildings and are used in large wall murals in restaurants.

Another area in which the obsessional art of mosaic-making is very much alive is in the work of 'outsider' artists. Working outside conventional art boundaries, these artists create visionary environments from broken and discarded china and are consequently becoming more widely known.

So we come back to this creative human drive, to recycle found and thrown away objects, and those with perhaps a sentimental value, to make sense of collections of stones and shells and to emphasize the significance of these modest and domestic elements in our lives. Whilst being aware of the fine artistic heritage of mosaics, we know

Left *The subtle natural tones of small shells make them a joy to work with.*

that it is also accessible to us and relevant to our current lives. We can use this historic medium in the same way as the Ancient Greeks and Romans, but we can also adapt, invent and add materials to make a truly contemporary craft form and one that has the advantage of permanence and durability. Mosaics can be used inside and out and as long as you are patient and willing to experiment with the medium, you will be amply rewarded for your efforts.

The connection with patchwork has been mentioned many times. The collecting of different materials, from close to home, gifts from friends, perhaps a sadly broken family heirloom, a treasured lustre plate or teapot, a collection of favourite pebbles or selected shells from a memorable seaside holiday – these are all gathered together and eventually recycled into a different form. Like a patchwork piecing all the disparate elements together, making an object that carries a trace of a former life, or signifies an experience or friendship in a permanent and decorative way, carries its own reward.

Above *A witty and elegant plate assembled from a patchwork of china pieces.*

Materials

Building up a collection of materials for use in mosaic work is rather similar to gathering a collection of materials for use in patchwork. The two crafts have similar origins as, with both, designs are created from carefully selected pieces that often carry sentimental meaning or fond memories. Maybe you will incorporate a treasured but sadly broken plate inherited from a grandmother, perhaps some pebbles or shells collected at the beach can be transformed and displayed at the same time (see pages 90, 94 and 116). Broken terracotta garden pots need not be hidden as shards for drainage at the base of planters, but instead cut, shaped and turned into paving slabs (see page 106).

Charity shops, markets and jumble sales are good sources for inexpensive china, and when your friends are aware that you are collecting broken china, you will be surprised how much you receive. Pretty rimmed plates and saucers, glinting lustre shards and coloured and patterned pieces, some antique and some contemporary – in a child-like way it is just like collecting treasure.

Right *A rainbow-coloured collection of mosaic materials, gathered over the years.*

Below *Shards of broken terracotta are ideal for outdoor use.*

Smalti, ceramic and glass tesserae, although specialist materials, are readily available from a mosaic supplier, but the joy of mosaics is that the beginner can start this exciting craft with no specialist materials and still make beautiful and unique pieces. Before starting to design projects, it is a good idea to sort all your found, collected and bought materials into individual containers, They look so beautiful that this can be a source of inspiration in itself.

Plate rims

Some plate, saucer, dish or cup rims are very beautiful, especially on older china. The repeated pattern is often gilded in a line against a rounded rim and can be cut out and used as a motif on its own. Junk shops, markets, jumble sales and charity shops are usually a good source. A number of projects in this book use rims to decorative advantage (see pages 34, 66 and 80).

Clockwise from

top right *Antique*

flower-patterned

china; classic

blue-and-white

designs; motifs and

lettering; the many

shades of white

china; decorated

plate rims;

sparkling

lustreware.

Blue-and-white china

Traditional blue-and-white china patterns such as the famous Chinese willow pattern are as popular today as they were hundreds of years ago. If you are lucky enough to find old plates, you will notice the patterns and glazes are often more subtle than contemporary pieces. These have been used to advantage in the projects on pages 58, 62 and 102.

Coloured china

When making mosaics it is very useful, not to say inspiring, to have a large selection of china pieces in many colours to incorporate into a design. These are ordinary broken household pieces gradually built up into a collection. If you are short of a particular colour, it can be worth buying an inexpensive piece of the right colour and breaking it up into appropriate-sized pieces. Coloured china is used on pages 34, 72, 80 and 112.

White china

White china shards are extremely useful as a background or for use as a contrastingly unpatterned section in a design (see pages 58, 102 and 120). Plain white china is extremely common and inexpensive to buy. It is occasionally thicker than patterned china and some adjustment will need to be made with the adhesive to make all the pieces the same level. The subtle range of whites can become an interesting part of your design.

Antique china

Antique china tends to be decorated with exquisitely patterned designs which are a joy to work with. The images are often hand-painted and we can only marvel at the skills employed in producing it in former times. The finer, higher fired pieces are usually known as porcelain and are a little more difficult to cut and shape, whereas china fired at a lower temperature is much easier to cut. See this china in use on pages 30 and 120.

Lustre

Glazed with real metals, even occasionally gold and silver, lustreware is often found in the shape of jugs, plates and tea services. It doesn't need to be antique, although lustreware was very popular in the 1930s and 40s. New pieces are easily available and you may need to buy a piece especially for a project (see page 44). Small elements of lustre strategically placed in a design can glitter and sparkle (see page 112) or glimmer as part of a rich design focusing the eye on a striking pattern (see page 66).

Patterned china

It is worth sorting out the broken china into small containers of different patterns so it is easy to find what you need. China with text makes an interesting image (see page 48) and motifs can be cut out of larger pieces to form key points in a design (see page 72). Black-and-white patterns make particularly striking elements in a design.

**Clockwise from
top right**
*Treasured
seashells;
shimmering glass
tesserae; coloured
china; matt ceramic
tesserae; jewel-like
glass smalti;
smooth sea-
washed pebbles.*

Terracotta shards

These are simply flower pots that are cracked or broken and are no longer any use in the garden. Cut and shape them with tile nippers into the required shapes and incorporate them into a design, perhaps contrasting with another element such as white pebbles (see page 108). They are easy to cut because the terracotta is fired at a low temperature.

Shells

It is quite surprising how many people already have a collection of shells even if they are gathering dust or hidden away in a cupboard. As well as gathering on seaside holidays (a favourite childhood activity) they can be bought from seaside gift shops or novelty shops which import them from all over the world. Once you start to study shells you realize the fascination of their myriad shapes, colours, sizes and patterns (see pages 90 and 116).

Pebbles

Pebbles, like shells, come in an extraordinary variety of colours, shapes and sizes. Buy them from home style shops and mosaic suppliers as well as garden centres, although this is a more expensive way to purchase them. Collect on country or beach walks, add to the ones you buy and you will soon have enough for a mosaic (see pages 94 and 108).

Ceramic tesserae

Ceramic tesserae, available in different sizes and in a large variety of colours, are intended for mosaic use. As they cut so easily, this is a rewarding material for a newcomer to mosaics to use. Of an even thickness, once they are stuck in place and grouted, the surface will be particularly even and smooth. They are consequently suitable for the oak leaf table top (page 22) and the tray (page 40).

Glass tesserae

This traditional mosaic material comes in an enormous variety of intense colours. They are easy to cut with tile nippers but care must be taken as the cutting produces tiny glass shards. Used uncut and with the colours sensitively arranged into a contemporary geometric pattern (see page 26), they create a stunning and vibrant effect. A more subtle approach of using them in conjunction with patterned china can be seen on page 98 or page 66, where the metallic lustre variety has been quartered and used to infill the design.

Smalti

Glass smalti, famously used in Byzantine mosaics, is the most stunning mosaic material. It is a pigmented glass which, in its molten state, has been poured into slabs and broken into uneven pieces. It was traditionally used closely packed without grout, creating a rich, light-reflective surface. With an intense colour and faceted surface, it makes a striking contrast when used with a quieter material such as ceramic tesserae (see page 86).

Basic Techniques

Although many mosaic techniques are clearly illustrated in the step-by-step photographs throughout this book, you may find it helpful to refer to this section to study them in closer detail. Mastering these techniques will prove particularly useful when you become more experienced and embark on your own designs.

There are two approaches to mosaic work – the direct and indirect methods. The direct method, used in most of the projects here, simply means sticking pieces of mosaic directly onto the backing material. This is most appropriate if you need to see the design developing, for example when using materials such as china and some tesserae where the front and back surfaces have a different appearance. The finished piece is usually grouted.

The indirect method is used in two of the projects – the wall panel on page 94 and the paving slab on page 108. Here the mosaic pieces are laid upside down in a wooden box mould lined with a layer of sand, and cement is poured over the design. When set, the slab is released from the mould and turned over to reveal the finished design. This method is often used when the materials are uneven in character, such as pebbles or pieces of terracotta. Laying them on the flat base of the mould assures an even surface.

Cutting

The wonderful thing about working with mosaics is that you really need no more than the invaluable tile nippers with which to cut and shape the pieces to the required shape. Straight lines can easily be cut by applying pressure at the edge of the piece, but it takes a little practice to cut more complicated curved edges. This is done by gently nibbling away at the edges of the piece. When using larger pieces such as plates or flowerpots, it is safest to place the items to be broken inside a plastic bag covered with a cloth. A few blows with a hammer break the items into more manageable sizes which can then be shaped with tile nippers.

1

Cutting glass tesserae into quarters

Use tile nippers to grip the tesserae halfway along one side. Squeeze the handles together tightly and the resulting pressure will break the square neatly in half. Cut each piece in half again to create quarters. Ceramic tesserae are cut in the same manner. To avoid the hazard of tiny glass fragments, tesserae can be cut under water in a bowl or bucket.

2

Shaping ceramic tesserae

To make an even curve, use the tile nippers to nibble away tiny sections of the square in turn, following a curve. If it helps, draw a guideline on the tile for you to follow. Take care as the tesserae will break if you try to cut off too much at a time.

3 **Cutting squares or rectangles from china**

China is cut in the same way as tesserae using tile nippers. China usually breaks evenly in a straight line from the point of pressure. The firing temperature of china or porcelain affects the way it cuts. Trial and error is the rule – some pieces will not do as you want and you may have to use the nibbling technique to achieve the required shape.

4 **Making triangular petal shapes**

These triangular pieces have been cut from the edge of a plain blue plate of low-fired china. Hold the tile nippers at a 45-degree angle from the edge of the plate, apply pressure to break the china, then repeat on the other side to make the triangular shape.

5 **Cutting out motifs from china**

Select pictorial motifs from cracked or broken pieces of china and use the tile nippers to nibble around the chosen image. It is important to work patiently and cut away small pieces at a time to avoid the china snapping across the chosen image.

6 **Cutting rim sections**

Old china plates, saucers and bowls often have beautiful rims and these can be used to great effect in mosaic work. First, use the tile nippers at right angles to the rim to cut the plate into sections measuring approximately 2 cm (¾ in) in length. Then place the nippers at right angles on the cut edge and cut parallel to the design on the rim .

Sticking

There are a number of different adhesives that can be used when making mosaics. The choice is partly influenced by the material used, the colour, its location and the backing material. Waterproof cement-based adhesives are generally ideal for outside work, although the combination tile-and-grout types can also be suitable. Water-resistant PVA glue is used particularly when the flat tesserae of even thickness are stuck to a wooden backing material (see page 26). A traditional cement mix is used when making slabs with the indirect method for outdoor use. Interior adhesives without cement may also be used and have the advantage of an extended drying time so adjustments can be made to the design as it is being worked on.

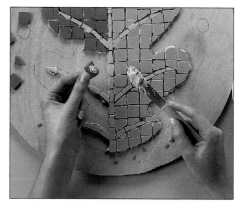

1 Buttering adhesive

Apply a small amount of the adhesive directly to the back of the tesserae with a small knife and press in position on the background. This method is particularly suitable when applying the mosaic onto a drawn design. It is also used when the pieces used are of differing thicknesses and the level can be adjusted by applying more or less adhesive.

2 Applying adhesive directly onto the background

Apply a small area of adhesive evenly to the background to be covered and push the tesserae into it, taking care not to allow the adhesive to squeeze up through the resulting gaps. This method is ideal for external work where an even thickness of tesserae is used or for covering a curved surface.

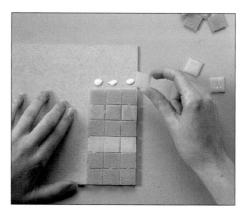

3 Using PVA as an adhesive

Apply waterproof PVA glue directly to a small area of the background material and push the evenly spaced tiles onto it, then repeat until the whole area is covered. Allow the adhesive to dry before grouting. This method is suitable for glass and ceramic tesserae that are uncut and of even thickness.

Grouting

Grouting means filling in the gaps between the mosaic pieces to give a smooth surface to the finished design. It also protects the mosaic from water and dirt. Exterior mosaics may be grouted with cement or cement-based powdered grout, which is available in black, grey and white. The latter is suitable for interior work as well. White grout can be coloured by adding a small quantity of water-based or acrylic paint. Dark grout brings out the intensity of colour of the mosaic pieces while grout of a similar tone has the effect of unifying the design. Ready mixed grout is useful in some cases and the combination tile adhesive/grout is necessary for projects such as those using shells as their uneven surfaces make it impossible to grout in the normal manner. Quickly sponge off excess grout and polish the dry piece with a cloth to remove any remaining traces.

Safety

• Always wear a face mask and protective goggles when cutting any kind of ceramic or glass pieces as fine dust and tiny glass shards result from the cutting and can be extremely hazardous.

• To avoid the danger of tiny glass fragments, tesserae can be held and cut under water in a bowl or bucket.

• Always keep your work space clean and wear a face mask even when sweeping the floor where you have been working to avoid breathing in the dust.

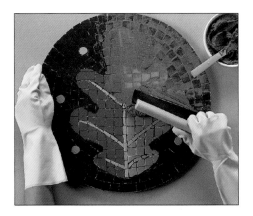

1 Applying grout

There are a number of ways to apply grout, depending on the size and surface of your mosaic. For a large flat surface a squeegee is ideal. Pull it across the surface, pushing the grout firmly down into the gaps. A palette or kitchen knife can be used on smaller items. This can also be done with fingers on uneven or curved surfaces.

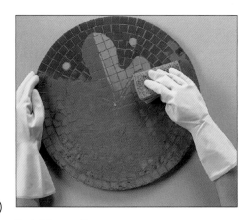

2 Rubbing off excess grout

After the grout begins to set (see packet for drying times), rub excess from the surface with a damp sponge or stiff nail brush. When dry, polish off any remaining film with a dry, lint-free cloth. Remove any residue of grout or cement adhesive with brick or patio cleaner. This is a diluted hydrochloric acid and packet instructions must be followed to the letter.

HOME DESIGN

Using the simple techniques involved in making mosaics you can be as adventurous or inventive as you like in creating beautiful and useful objects to enhance your home.

Oak Leaf Table

This charming metal side table has been decorated using subtly coloured matt ceramic tiles. A large number of tiles need to be cut to create the design but this is surprisingly easy with spring-loaded tile nippers. Rather than gluing the tiles directly onto the metal tabletop, they have been stuck onto a circle of varnished plywood, the edge of which has been cleverly disguised with a strip of scalloped lead. As well as being decorative, the lead acts as a rim, making it unnecessary to screw the surface onto the metal beneath.

The quantities of materials given here are for a table 40 cm (16 in) in diameter. You can alter the quantities of tiles according to the size of the table you wish to decorate. It is useful to have a spare piece of board for sketching the design and laying out the tiles. You can then apply the adhesive and transfer them one by one to the actual plywood tabletop.

Materials

Folding metal table

Piece of plywood 9 mm (³⁄₈ in) thick, cut into 40 cm diameter (16 in) circle

Spare piece of board

Template (see page 124)

Pencil

Ceramic tiles 2 cm (³⁄₄ in) square, one 30 cm (12 in) square sheet in each of blue, yellow and light and dark grey

Tile nippers

Face mask and goggles

Ready-to-use waterproof tile adhesive

Small knife

Bowl

Powdered grout

Brown acrylic paint

Rubber squeegee

Sponge

Rubber gloves

Soft polishing cloth

1 Draw around the circle of plywood with the pencil onto the spare board. Working on the spare board, place the oak leaf template in the centre of this circle and draw around with pencil. Draw three small equidistant circles on each side of the leaf and set aside. Now place the template centrally on the plywood circle, draw around and add the smaller circles as before.

2 Using the tile nippers and wearing the face mask and goggles, cut and shape a number of the yellow tiles to make the leaf veins. Place them in the centre of the leaf on the spare board. Cut the light grey tiles to fit around the veins on one side of the leaf. Repeat the process on the other side using the blue tiles. Try to keep the vertical and horizontal joins between the tiles even – this is important for neatness and also means you need to cut fewer tiles.

3 When the design is complete on the spare board, transfer and stick each piece in place on the plywood circle. Start with the veins, smearing a small quantity of adhesive on the back of each tile and pressing it into position, leaving a gap of about 2 mm (¹⁄₁₆ in) between each tile. The adhesive should not squeeze up between the joins as you need space for grouting.

4 Continue in this manner and stick the light grey and blue tiles onto the leaf outline, buttering each tile with adhesive before sticking in place. At this point it may be necessary to make some adjustments to the shapes with the tile nippers, especially as you need to make sure that you leave a small gap between each join.

5 Use the tile nippers to cut six circular yellow tiles and stick them in place onto the previously drawn circles. Stick a line of the dark grey tiles all around the edge of the circle, then fill in the rest of the background, cutting the tiles to shape where they meet the leaf and the yellow circles.

6 Allow the adhesive to dry overnight. Mix the grout in a bowl following the packet instructions and add a small quantity of acrylic paint to achieve the desired shade of brown. Spread the grout over the tiles using the rubber squeegee, working it well into the joins (you may wish to wear rubber gloves for this step). Leave for about 30 minutes so that it begins to set.

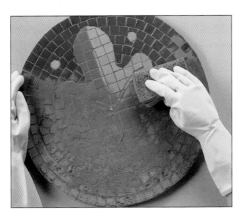

7 Using a clean, damp sponge, wipe off all the excess grout from the top of the mosaic, taking care not to pull the grout out from between the tiles.

8 Wait another 30 minutes to allow the remaining grout to dry, then polish the surface of the table with a soft cloth. This helps to remove any grout residue from the tiles (this is more likely to collect on matt ceramic tiles than on glazed ones).

Bathroom Splashback

This vibrantly coloured project is solely inspired by the extraordinary selection of colours available in glass tesserae. The translucent quality of the pigment in the glass means that the colours have a particular intensity and, as with all design using colour, the choice of juxtapositions is vital to the final effect.

This easy project involves no cutting as the pattern is created with the use of changing colours. The only skill involved is trying to ensure that the spaces between the tesserae are as even as possible. This approach can be extended to cover a whole bathroom wall, but if you feel a little less adventurous, try decorating a simple tabletop.

Why not decorate your entire bathroom taking a colour from the tesserae pattern as your inspiration. Extend this colour matching to choice of towels and even your toothbrushes!

Materials

Piece of plywood or MDF (medium density fibreboard) 4 mm (¼ in) thick, cut to fit above the basin

Waterproof PVA adhesive

Selection of coloured glass tesserae in the tones used here, or your choice of colours

Grey grout

Palette knife

Sponge

Soft polishing cloth

1 Put small dots of glue directly onto the background material and start to build up a column of turquoise tesserae three tiles wide. It is most important to make sure that the pieces are evenly spaced with about 2 mm (¹⁄₁₆ in) between each piece.

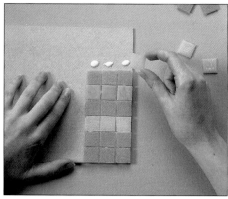

2 After the first two rows, add a row of pale blue followed by bands of turquoise, pink, turquoise, acid yellow and complete the column with two rows of turquoise.

3 Stick a second column of green tiles in place interspersed with a deeper turquoise, blue-green and a strong orange. Start the third column using pale blue banded first with pale pink, then with strong orange and finally grey-green.

4 Continue working in this way adding three-tile-wide columns in subtle tones and contrasts. Allow the glue to dry and grout and polish in the normal way (see page 19). To fix the splashback to the wall, use cement adhesive and grout to finish around the edges.

Number Plaque

This pretty and practical mosaic number plaque is made using ceramic and glass tesserae as well as specially shaped china pieces. Many of the projects in this book use combinations of materials and this is one of the most satisfying to make. The three-dimensional effect on the number five is created using two tones of green to mimic a shadow (a traditional mosaic technique) and the leaves on the wreath are carefully cut from a rather special, old Japanese plate. A sense of satisfaction is achieved when a favourite piece of china that has been accidentally broken can be reassembled into another long-lasting form.

MDF (medium density fibreboard) has been used as a backing material and can be varnished to protect against damp, but if you want to incorporate the plaque into an outside wall, it would be better to make the design on a large ceramic tile.

Materials

Felt pen

Sheet of scrap paper

Scissors

Dinner plate or compass

Piece of MDF (medium density fibreboard) 25 cm (10 in) square, 1 cm (½ in) thick

6 pale green and 18 dark green glass tesserae

Tile nippers

Face mask and goggles

Waterproof PVA adhesive

24 leaves cut from a green patterned plate

100 white matt ceramic tesserae

Grey grout

Bowl

Palette knife

Sponge

Lint-free polishing cloth

1 Draw or copy your chosen number onto a piece of paper and cut out. Draw around a plate or use a compass to mark a circle 19 cm (7½ in) in diameter centrally on the background board. Place the template in the middle and draw around it.

2 Wearing a face mask and goggles, cut the pale green tesserae with the tile nippers into quarters and stick in place on the number using the PVA. Some special cutting will be necessary to match the design. Leave a space along all the right-hand edges and below the horizontal line at the top.

3 Cut some smaller dark green pieces and fit into the spaces around the number to work as the shadow. Don't worry if these are not a perfect fit as the grout will unify the design.

4 Cut the remaining dark green tesserae into strips approximately 4 mm (¼ in) wide. (You should be able to cut three from each tessera, although it is inevitable they will not all cut evenly.) Stick in place around the marked circle.

5 Set out all the leaf shapes that you have previously cut (see page 17) evenly around the circle in pairs and stick into place as shown.

6 Allow the glue to dry so that pieces are all secure before sticking the background of white ceramic tesserae in place. Use tile nippers to cut the pieces into quarters and begin by sticking them around the number in the middle, then work outwards, cutting and shaping the pieces to fit as you go. Fill in the remaining areas and allow the glue to dry thoroughly.

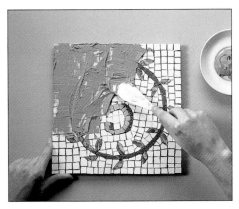

7 Mix up the grey grout to a stiff consistency and apply with a palette knife, working the grout well into the gaps. Leave for a few minutes before wiping off the excess with a barely damp sponge.

8 Leave the plaque to dry for an hour, then vigorously polish off any remaining grout with a lint-free cloth.

Butterfly Tiles

These exquisite butterfly tiles could be used singly as pot stands or as wall tiles in a kitchen or bathroom. The butterfly itself has been created by setting specially cut pieces of coloured and patterned antique china into a contrasting matt black background. Although the background is flat, the china pieces are of varying thicknesses and need to be fixed in place with a tile adhesive to create more bulk in order to bring all the tile pieces up to one level. Try to use china with motifs such as flowers and leaves that can be used on each wing. Patterned plate rims have been used effectively in combination with a contrasting colour along the insect's body.

The shape of a butterfly is a perfect way to exploit the idea of symmetry. It is extremely easy to make your own template as each side is identical – just draw half a butterfly onto a folded piece of paper (with the body on the fold line), cut out with scissors and open up the fold to reveal the entire design.

Materials

Template (see page 124)

Black ceramic tile, 15 cm (6 in) square

White pencil

Sheet of white paper

Pencil

Face mask

Tile nippers

Selection of broken antique china in plain colours and patterns, flower and leaf motifs, and plate rims

Ceramic adhesive

Small bowl

Kitchen knife

Tweezers

Matt black ceramic mosaic tiles

Black grout

Palette knife

Craft knife

Sponge

Rubber gloves

Soft polishing cloth

1 Place the template centrally on the black ceramic tile and draw around it with the white pencil. Draw around the template again, this time using the pencil on the sheet of white paper.

2 Wearing a face mask and goggles, cut out oval-shaped motifs from the china plates (here flowers have been chosen for the top wings and leaves for the lower). You will need to nibble around the designs carefully to make the shapes you require. Place them in position on the sheet of paper.

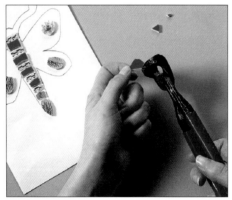

3 Cut a leaf motif for the end of the body and cut strips of pink and patterned plate rim to make alternate stripes on the body. Continue building up the butterfly design in this way on the paper pattern. Cut green strips for the antennae and little star motifs to place at the end of these. Cut pieces for the wings from patterned china plates. If available, use lined patterns to simulate the veining on the wings.

4 Next, carefully transfer the pre-cut pieces one by one from the paper to the tile, coating the back of each piece with enough adhesive to make it even and level with all the other pieces. Start with the body and the wing motifs.

5 When fitting the wing pieces together, you may need to use tweezers to place the smaller ones correctly. You may also find that some more cutting or adjusting needs to be done at this stage for a neat finish. As before, always try to make each new piece level with the last so the finished surface will be as even as possible.

6 When the butterfly design is complete, cut the matt black tiles into quarters and stick evenly in place as the background. Nibble the edges to fit neatly around the curved edges of the butterfly. Gently wipe off any excess adhesive from the surface and leave to dry.

7 Mix up some black grout according to the packet instructions and, wearing rubber gloves, grout the entire surface and around the edges of the tile, using the palette knife and pushing the grout well into the gaps.

8 Leave for a few minutes and very gently wipe off the excess grout with an almost dry damp sponge. You may need to clean grout from the china shards using a pointed craft knife to reveal as much of the glazed surface of the china as possible. Leave to dry, then polish with a clean cloth.

Cup-and-Saucer Tray

The base of this useful slope-sided wooden tray has been decorated with a cleanly drawn cup-and-saucer design. The ceramic tiles used for this project mean that the tray can be used to carry hot dishes and is, of course, impervious to water.

Ceramic mosaic tiles come in a large variety of colours and are extremely easy to cut, thus providing an ideal medium for the beginner. As the tray base is completely flat and the tiles are even in thickness, it is sensible and far simpler to fix the tiles in place with a waterproof PVA adhesive and grout over this. Grey grout has been used for this project to add cohesion to the design as it is tonally closer to the colours used.

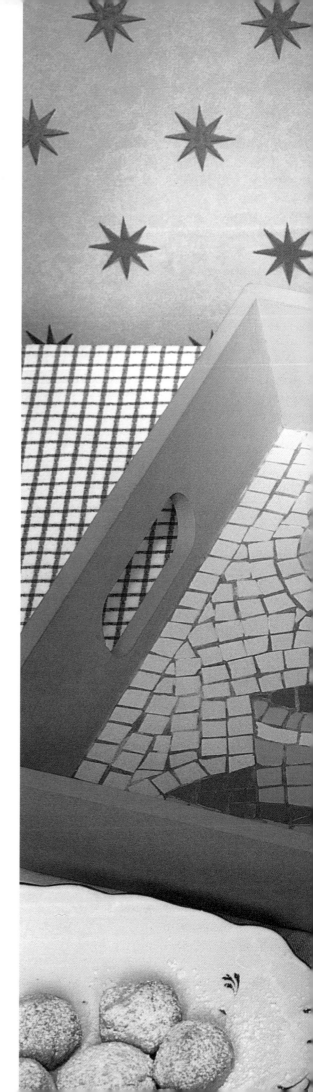

Materials

Templates (see page 125)

Black pen

4 sheets of white paper

Thick red marker pen

Slope-sided wooden tray – this one has a base 30 x 44 cm (12 x 17¼ in) and sides 7 cm (2¾ in) deep

Unglazed, matt ceramic mosaic tiles, 2.5 cm (1 in) square, 5 mm (¼ in) thick (approximately 20 yellow, 20 pink, 20 turquoise, 20 dark grey-green, 25 light grey-green, 15 tan, and 250 or one sheet for the background)

Tile nippers

Face mask and goggles

PVA adhesive

Grey grout

Bowl

Palette knife

Rubber squeegee

Sponge

Baltic blue acrylic paint

Paintbrush

1 Position the templates on the base of the tray and neatly draw around them with the black pen. Add the detail of the inner markings. Also draw around the templates on the white paper and mark up with the red pen.

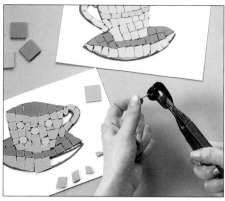

2 Wearing a face mask and goggles, cut each tile into four and shape further to make up the design on the templates as shown. The pink spots are made by nibbling a circular shape from each quartered tile. The tiles fitted around these spots will need to be cut carefully to fit.

3 When all the cups have been assembled on the paper templates, start to transfer them onto the drawn cups on the base of the tray. Put a little glue onto the wooden base and gently slide each piece into place. You may need to do some extra cutting at this point for a neat design.

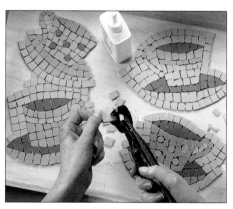

4 Cut the background tiles into quarters as you use them. Start off by surrounding the teacup shapes, cutting the tiles to fit as you go. Work your way outwards from each cup, filling in the space between by cutting the tiles specially. Continue in the same way, aiming to finish with a straight line around the edge of the base. Allow the glue to dry.

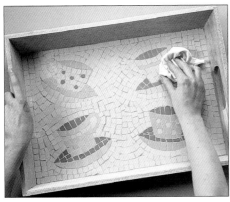

5 Mix up the grey grout and apply with the palette knife, pressing it firmly into the cracks. Leave for a few minutes, then wipe off the excess with the squeegee. Clean the base with an almost dry sponge and polish with a cloth when dry.

6 Paint the raised sides off the tray with at least two coats of the acrylic paint, allowing it to dry between coats.

Silver-lined Bowl

This unusual idea of lining a ready-made bowl with shards of silver lustre porcelain is very effective. The light reflects off the many-faceted surface of the interior of the bowl, providing a rich contrast with the plain blue of the outside surface. The white grout has been gilded with easy-to-apply silver gilt cream which enhances the richness of the silver shards.

Lustre cups and saucers were specially bought to use for this project as lustreware is uncommon and it is unlikely that you will have any in your accumulating collection of broken china. However, older examples of lustreware have a subtler quality and are less brash than the pieces used here. A group of small bowls decorated in this manner and filled with exotic sweets would grace a festive table.

lustreware have a subtler quality and are less brash than the pieces used here. A group of small bowls decorated in this manner and filled with exotic sweets would grace a festive table.

Materials

Silver lustre china (one coffee cup and two matching saucers were used here)

Tile nippers

Face mask and goggles

All-in-one tile and grout adhesive

Kitchen knife

Small bowl

China bowl 8 cm (3¼ in) high, 5 cm (2 in) base diameter and 14 cm (5½ in) diameter at top

Sponge

Craft knife

Soft polishing cloth

Silver gilt cream

Two small cloths for applying and polishing gilt cream

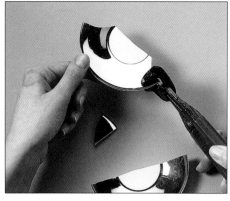

1 Use the tile nippers to break the porcelain up into small, irregular pieces (wear a face mask and goggles whilst doing this). Separate the pieces from around the rim of the saucer and the cup in order to use them around the rim of the bowl.

2 Coat the back of each little piece with the adhesive and place very carefully, jigsaw-style, in the base of the bowl. Then begin to build the patchwork pattern up the sides of the bowl. As the pieces of porcelain vary in thickness depending on which part of the cup or saucer they are cut from, adjust the amount of adhesive to create an even surface.

3 When you reach the top of the bowl, use the pieces that you set aside from the rims of the porcelain, matching these rims against the edge of the bowl. This makes a smooth·and neat edge. Smooth and neaten any adhesive visible between the silver pieces and the bowl beneath and clean off any that has smeared accidentally onto the silver surface. Allow to dry.

4 Use the same mixture to grout the surface, using the knife to press it well into the gaps, and leave for a few minutes.

5 With an almost dry sponge, remove excess grout from the surface. For a really neat finish, you may need to use a craft knife to remove any grout that the sponge failed to reach. Sponge along the top of the rim. Leave the grout to dry completely, then polish with a clean, dry cloth.

6 Apply the gilt cream to small sections of the bowl. Polish to remove the excess with a clean cloth and repeat this process until all the grout on the interior of the bowl is shining.

Teapot Stand

Every kitchen needs a teapot stand or tablemat to protect vulnerable surfaces from heat and this chequered tile is the perfect solution. The tile is wittily appropriate to a kitchen environment as the design is made up of the china factory marks found on the underside of plates. Older plates have very interesting motifs featuring flowers, crowns and decorative text identifying the maker of the pottery concerned. The striking checked pattern has been made simply by contrasting the china marks with matt black ceramic tesserae.

Second-hand and charity shops are a good source of cheap china if you don't have enough suitable broken china of your own, and if following this design, remember that it doesn't matter what the plate looks like as you only need the marked underside. If you find it difficult to assemble enough china to provide you with the right number of marks, intersperse these with striking patterned motifs. A number of such tiles would make an interesting design on a kitchen wall behind the work surface.

Materials

Tile nippers

Face mask and goggles

18 plates, saucers, etc, with interesting china marks

18 black matt ceramic tesserae

Black glazed ceramic tile 15 cm (6 in) square

Pencil

Paper or board slightly larger than the ceramic tile

Cement-based adhesive

Bowl

Small knife

Black grout

Sponge

Polishing cloth

1 Use the tile nippers to cut out the china marks from the centre of the plates (wear a face mask and goggles for this). Don't worry if you accidentally cut the mark in half – the resulting pieces can become part of the design. Make each square approximately the same size as the matt black tesserae.

2 Draw around the tile with the pencil onto the paper or board and arrange your pattern of china marks and tiles on the area marked. Balance the design so that similar marks are well spaced out.

3 Turn the black tile glazed side down and stick your pre-arranged pattern onto the tile, buttering the back of each piece as you go. Vary the amount of adhesive used on the back of each piece to ensure an even finished surface.

4 To keep the gaps between all the pieces even, lay vertical and horizontal lines at the same time. Don't allow the adhesive to squeeze up through the gaps. Leave to dry overnight, then grout and polish (see page 19).

Use a variation of this chequerboard design to create your own chess board. It would look especially good with a contrasting patterned border surrounding the squares.

GIFTS

There is nothing more appreciated than a well-thought-out and carefully hand-made gift, and one of the beauties of mosaic work is that it will last for ever, perhaps as a sign of an enduring friendship.

Victorian Boots

These elegant little stand-up boots are inspired by the decorative Victorian brass boots which are still collected today. They were usually displayed on a mantel shelf with a box of matches for the fire hidden behind them. You may like to use them for the same purpose and need only stick your box of matches onto the back of the boot. When the matches run out, simply insert another slot-in section as a renewed source of matches.

As the surface onto which the mosaic tiles are stuck is completely flat, it is simpler and more sensible to stick the quartered tiles in place with waterproof PVA glue. As the tiles used are light in colour, white grout has been used for this project and the edges of the boots carefully painted with white paint to match. If you wish to make a matching pair, turn the template over when cutting out the second boot.

Materials

Template (see page 126)

Marker pen

Piece of MDF (medium density fibreboard) 16 x 25 cm (6¼ x 10 in), 6 mm (¼ in) thick

Jigsaw

Face mask and goggles

Piece of MDF (medium density fibreboard), 4 x 8 cm (1½ x 3¼ in), to use as a support

Ceramic mosaic tiles in pink, white and buff colours

Waterproof PVA glue

Tile nippers

White grout

Palette knife

Sponge

Soft polishing cloth

White paint and a brush

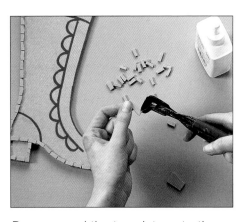

1 Draw around the template onto the MDF and cut out neatly with a jigsaw (always wear a face mask and goggles when cutting MDF). Draw the detail of the design onto the boot with the marker pen. Using the nippers, cut each buff-coloured tile in half and then cut each half into five short sections. Glue in place around the perimeter of the boot, at the curved line at the heel, across the top of the heel and at the top of the boot.

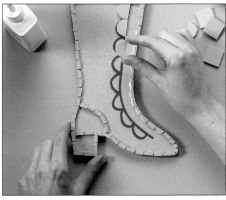

2 Cut the pink tiles into scallop shapes with the tile nippers, nibbling away small pieces at a time to make even curves. Stick them in place on the marked areas.

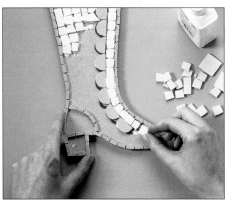

3 Cut the white tiles into quarters and fill all the remaining areas as shown. You will need to cut some shapes to fit neatly around the curved pink tiles.

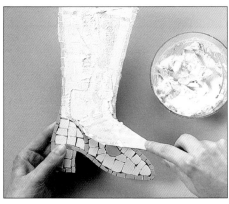

4 Mix the white grout according to the packet instructions and, using the palette knife, smooth and press firmly over the surface. Remember to grout the sides of the boot.

5 After five minutes wipe away the excess grout with a barely damp sponge. Leave the grout to dry, then polish with a dry cloth.

6 Stick the MDF stand onto the back of the heel, making sure it is positioned so the boot stands upright. When dry, carefully paint the back and sides of the boot with white paint.

The flat, cut-out images of a pair of boots are designed specifically to adorn a mantel shelf. As you become more confident, the design idea can be extended to other shapes such as cats or vases of flowers.

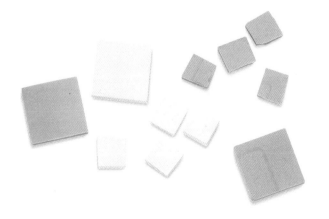

China Shard Bird

This challenging project is quite adventurous and is a humorous play on the china figures popular in the eighteenth and nineteenth centuries and made in Staffordshire, England. Animals were a great favourite, particularly the matching pairs of dogs in varying sizes that were so often displayed on a mantel shelf or sitting sentry either side of the hearth.

This chunky bird has been made by covering a wooden bird-shaped blank with a collection of old blue-and-white china in a simple but striking design. The difficulty comes when trying to achieve a level finish when using different thicknesses of broken china over a curved surface. Some of the china used here, particularly the blue-patterned pieces, have been dug up over the years whilst gardening and saved as local treasure in flowerpots and on potting shed shelves. So you see, the finished bird can tell a story as it sits on your windowsill.

Materials

Wooden bird blank approximately 35 cm (14 in) long, 20 cm (8 in) high and 9 cm (3½ in) wide

Marker pen

Selection of old broken china in blue-and-white and plain white

Face mask and goggles

Tile nippers

Adhesive

Kitchen knife

Small bowl

White grout

Palette knife

Sponge

Soft polishing cloth

Craft knife

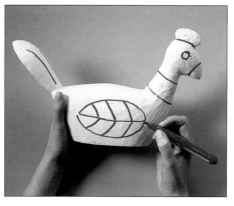

1 Using the thick marker pen, draw the guidelines for the wing, collar, tail, eye, beak and comb on the wooden bird. Try to make both sides of the bird symmetrical.

2 Wearing a face mask and goggles and using tile nippers, cut the blue-and-white china into small rectangular lengths, smear the backs with adhesive and stick them in place over the marker lines on the wings. You will need to nibble the pieces a little to fit them neatly together.

3 Carefully nibble some small circular 'spots' and stick in place as an evenly spaced pattern around the body of the bird.

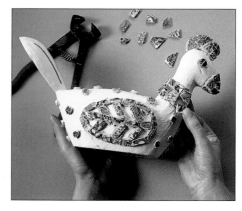

4 Now add two bands of blue-and-white china around the neck. Also cover the beak and the comb at the top of the head. Cut two more small circles and position as eyes. Try to make sure all the pieces achieve a similar finished level.

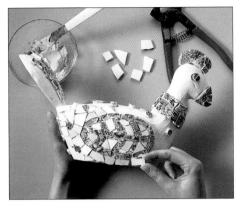

5 Add three lines of rectangular blue-and-white pieces along the front of the tail. Now fill in all the remaining areas, except the underside of the tail, with a random selection of white china. Although you are making a crazy patchwork, you will still need to cut some pieces for a neater fit. On the smaller curved areas such as the head, cut the pieces much smaller for a smoother, more rounded finish.

6 Now cover the underside of the tail with small, rectangular pieces of blue-and-white china. Remove any excess adhesive from the surface and allow to dry before grouting.

7 Using a palette knife, apply the white grout firmly and evenly all over the surface of the bird, working it well into the cracks. Leave for a few minutes.

8 Wipe off the excess grout gently with an almost dry sponge, taking care not to pull any out of the cracks. Finally, polish with a clean, dry cloth, removing any stubborn dry grout with a craft knife if necessary.

Inlaid Box

Antique blue-and-white china shards cut from broken plates and set into a highly polished papier mâché lid turn an everyday cardboard container into a jewellery box to be treasured. This has been gessoed and painted, then waxed and polished to give the finished box a rich patina to complement the treasured china pieces.

Gesso is a primer paint made from rabbit skin size and whiting and, after a number of applications, takes on the appearance and texture of ivory. It consequently makes a perfect ground for painting on. It is an ancient recipe and although it is possible to buy ready-made gesso from a good art shop, it is much better and quite an achievement to make your own.

Place two tablespoons of rabbit skin size in a bowl and add 300 ml (10 fl oz) of water. Leave overnight to dissolve. By morning it will have set like a jelly. Place the bowl over a saucepan of heated water to melt the size. Add the whiting spoon by spoon to the size, mixing well until the gesso has the consistency of cream. Use the gesso while it is still hot.

Materials

6 pieces of blue-and-white china

Face mask and goggles

Tile nippers

Piece of corrugated cardboard measuring 15 x 9 cm (6 x 3½ in)

Pen

Craft knife

PVA adhesive

Papier mâché box with lid approximately 15 x 9 cm (6 x 3½ in), 7.5 cm (3 in) high

Wallpaper paste

Bowl

Recycled paper

Gesso

2 paintbrushes

Fine 0000 gauge steel wool or very fine sandpaper

Blue acrylic paint

Wax polish

Two soft rags for polishing

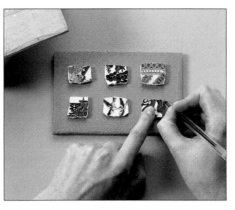

1 Wearing a face mask and goggles, cut six pieces of blue-and-white china into rectangles measuring 3 x 2 cm (1¼ x ¾ in). Place them, evenly spaced, on the piece of cardboard and draw around them with a pen.

2 Remove the china pieces and, using a craft knife, carefully cut away the marked areas to approximately the depth of the china shards.

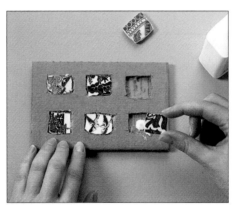

3 Squeeze some glue into each cut-away space and push the china piece in so that it is almost level with the surface (it can stand slightly proud as the level will be built up with the application of gesso).

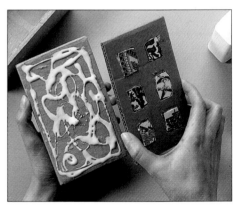

4 Cover the original lid of the box with glue and stick the new inlaid lid directly on top of this. Press firmly to make all areas adhere. Wipe away any excess glue that squeezes out.

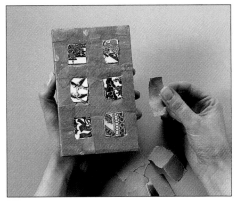

5 Mix the wallpaper paste according to packet instructions and tear the recycled paper into small pieces. Smear paste onto both sides of the paper and onto the surface of the cardboard. Paste the paper in place over the top, sides and underneath of the new, thicker lid. Smooth the paper with fingers to expel any air bubbles.

6 Allow the paper to dry. Mix the gesso (see page 62) and paint the surface of the box and lid around the china pieces as shown. Paint on four coats of gesso, allowing it to dry in between each coat. After the last coat is dry, scrape off any gesso that accidentally covers the china and rub the surface with fine steel wool or sandpaper to make a smooth surface. Wear a mask whilst doing this.

7 Mix the paint with water to a creamy consistency and paint over the box (leave the inside unpainted) and lid, carefully painting around the inlaid china. You will need to apply two coats to achieve the correct depth of colour. Allow the paint to dry.

8 Apply the polish with a rag, leave to dry for a few minutes and polish the wax off very vigorously with a clean rag. The box may be treated like wood and polish can be applied from time to time to enhance the patina.

Mosaic Plate

This charming, antique-looking plate is a kind of joke! A new and consequently unique design has been created from a number of broken plates. This is a perfect way of re-using and displaying treasured china that has been accidentally cracked or broken. It is also an ideal project with which to practise cutting intentional shapes that can be neatly pieced together.

A variety of china has been used here. Plain colours have been contrasted with highly patterned pieces, and a strong motif, in this case emphasizing the theme of rosebuds, has been used as the centre of the design. the plate is expertly and rather cleverly finished off with alternate segments of rims collected from two other plates. A simple round plate with a curved rim has been used as a base for sticking the pieces on, but there is no reason why you shoudn't be more adventurous and work on different-shaped backgrounds such as an oval or something more decoratively shaped.

Materials

Tile nippers

Assorted china in yellow, white, flower-patterned, rosebud design and two plates for the rim

Face mask and goggles

White tile adhesive

Bowl

Small knife

China plate, diameter 20 cm (8 in)

Grey grout

Palette knife

Sponge

Soft polishing cloth

1 Wearing a face mask and goggles, use the tile nippers to cut a central circular motif of roses and stick in the middle of the white plate by buttering the back with adhesive. (Refer to page 17 for instructions on how to cut specific shapes.)

2 Make a circle around this central motif using alternate pieces of plain yellow and a gold plate rim. If the china pieces are of varying thicknesses, adjust the amount of adhesive on the backs to obtain a level surface.

3 At this stage it is important to cut all the radiating wedge-shaped pieces before sticking any in place to make sure the design is symmetrical. You will need six flower-patterned, six yellow and twelve white pieces in total. Stick evenly in place as shown.

4 Cut about 36 1 cm (½ in) square pieces of pink rose-patterned china and stick them in place as a border around the radiating design.

5 Cut sections of rim from two different plates (a gold and rosebud design) 2 cm (¾ in) long and deep enough to fill the space left up to the rim of the base plate. Stick carefully in place, making sure the rounded edge of the cut rims just covers the rim of the base plate. Wipe off any excess adhesive from the surface and allow the plate to dry overnight.

6 Mix up the grey grout to a fairly stiff consistency and work well into the gaps between the pieces with the palette knife. Leave for a few minutes and wipe off the excess with a damp sponge. Allow to dry, then polish with a soft cloth.

Picture Frame

The really unique thing about the design of this frame is that the top curved section has been rescued from a rather valuable, artist-designed plate. A disastrous breakage has been mitigated by the fact that part of the plate can still take pride of place on the wall.

The subtle range of yellow 'tiles' has been cut to shape from an assortment of yellow china plates and mugs and an earthenware jug. The stencilled star motifs have been rescued from some much-loved French peasant soup plates. All have been stuck onto a wide ready-made frame.

The possibilities for using china mosaic in this way are endless, but to make a satisfying design keep the colour and pattern contrasts simple. The combination of order in the placing of the stars and the randomness of the yellow tiles is particularly effective here.

Materials

Patterned plate with an unbroken bold central section

Tile nippers

Face mask and goggles

Picture frame 20 cm (8 in) square with 8 cm (3¼ in) square opening

China with star motifs

Selection of broken china in various shades of yellow

All-in-one white tile and grout adhesive

Small bowl

Kitchen knife

Soft polishing cloth

1

Wearing a face mask and goggles and using tile nippers, gently nibble around the large motif to produce an even curved edge. (This takes some practice and you may need to experiment on less special pieces to perfect the technique – the trick is not to be impatient and try to take away too much at a time.) Luckily the central section of the plate shown here broke along the straight line.

2

Smear some adhesive on the back of the large china piece and press it into place centrally on the top of the picture frame. Leave a gap below it to allow space for a row of smaller yellow china.

3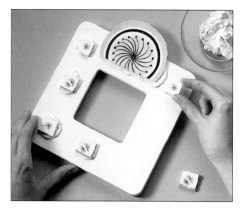

Cut seven star motifs (or similar) approximately 2 cm (¾ in) square and stick them in place on the frame so there are three along each side and one placed centrally on the base.

4

Cut a selection of the varied yellow china into square and rectangular pieces and stick them onto the frame in a random fashion around the star motifs. As you stick them in place, try to ensure the levels are compatible. The frame used here has rounded corners so these pieces have been nibbled to fit. Grout and polish in the normal manner (see page 19).

Chequered Vase

Like the bathroom splashback on page 26, this simple but extremely contemporary project requires no cutting of tiles or china. Consequently it is really quick to make.

Due to the simplicity of the design it is essential that the execution is neat and the gaps between the ceramic tiles are even and consistent. To feel secure about your choice of design it is important to work out the colour, tonal and compositional elements beforehand and much fun can be had at this stage. It is interesting to realize that some arrangements seem to fit and others just don't manage to work together. Trial and error is the only way to resolve this.

The tiles have been fixed to a plain, dark brown 'tank' vase with flat sides. Luckily this shape is readily available in home-style shops, florists and department stores.

Materials

Ceramic tank vase, approximately 12 cm (4¾ in) square and 21 cm (8½ in) high

Sheet of white paper

Pencil

Assortment of matt ceramic tiles – I used 36 pink, 28 yellow, 12 ochre, 32 brown, 24 buff and 24 grey

Cement-based adhesive

Bowl

Small knife

Black grout

Palette knife

Sponge

Soft polishing cloth

1 Lay the vase down sideways on a piece of paper and draw around the long side with the pencil. Start to build up your design on the drawn area, balancing the colour and tone carefully.

2 After you have worked out your design, mix the adhesive and apply the tiles by buttering the backs with adhesive. Don't use too much or it will squeeze out into the gaps between the tiles. Start with the horizontal line along the base of the vase.

3 Stick the vertical line up the left-hand edge of the vase to ensure the spacing will be equal over the whole design. Allow the tiles to stand slightly proud over the long edges. Cover the three other sides in the same manner, allowing the adhesive on each side to harden a little before going on to the next. Leave to dry overnight.

4 Mix the black grout and work well into the gaps using the palette knife. Wait a few minutes before wiping off the excess with a damp sponge. When the grout is dry, polish with a cloth. Dark grout can stain the matt tiles, but it can be removed with diluted hydrochloric acid (see page 19 and follow instructions on the container).

You may like to extend the project by using a combination of elements in the design, perhaps adding the contrast of a richly patterned piece of shaped china used sparingly against the matt tones of the ceramic tiles. The possibilities are endless.

Mosaic Spheres

Although the curved surface of a small sphere can be more difficult to work on than a flat surface, the finished result is quite stunning. These many-faceted balls are lovely to look at and a pleasure to hold. The possibilities of design are endless but it is worth starting with a simple structured design such as the one shown here.

The criss-cross patterns intersecting the ball into eight have been created using small sections of decorated plate rims (these are most often striped, cross-hatched or Greek key pattern) – you will start to see plate rims in a different light when working on these spheres! The remaining eight sections are infilled with lustrous glass tesserae cut into quarters. The larger sphere shown overleaf has motifs cut from the china set into the centre of these sections. The black grout gives the design a cohesive feel.

Materials

Wooden ball, 8 cm (3¼ in) diameter

Black marker pen

Plates and saucers with decorated rims

Tile nippers

Face mask and goggles

Adhesive

Small bowl

Kitchen knife

Pink lustre glass tesserae

Rubber gloves

Black grout

Filling knife

Sponge

Craft knife

Soft polishing cloth

1 Using the marker pen, draw a line around the circumference of the ball. Intersect this at right angles with another line, turn the ball slightly and draw another line dissecting the first two. This divides the sphere into eight even sections.

2 Each of these lines is decorated with a different plate rim. Using the tile nippers and wearing a face mask and goggles, cut small sections of the rim into lengths of approximately 1 cm (½ in) – you will need approximately 20 pieces per line.

3 Put a little adhesive onto the back of each cut piece and stick in place along the marked line. You can vary or break up the pattern by turning alternate pieces as you stick them down.

4 Holding the sphere carefully, repeat this procedure on the second line with a different-patterned rim. Repeat again with another pattern for the third line. Allow to dry a little, but make sure you don't leave any adhesive oozing out from underneath the applied pieces as this will make it difficult to stick the glass tesserae in place.

5 Cut the glass tesserae with the tile nippers into quarters and fit into the remaining sections. You will need to shape the central pieces to fit. Try to make sure that the tesserae are level with the china pieces and that the gaps between are evenly spaced.

6 Wearing rubber gloves, mix the black grout and press well into the gaps using a knife. Leave for a few minutes before wiping away the excess grout with an almost dry sponge. You may need to scrape extra grout away with a pointed craft knife for a really neat finish. Allow to dry, then polish with a clean cloth.

MOSAIC GARDEN

The durable quality of all kinds of mosaic work – whether it uses china shards, ceramic or glass tesserae, stones or pebbles – makes it ideally suited for outdoor or garden use.

Bird Bath

This unusual patterned bird bath has been cleverly made inside an upturned dustbin lid. The handle on the underside means that it is easy to balance on a bed of pebbles set in the earth or to settle in the top of a decorative chimney pot column.

Simple overlapping arcs created from strongly pigmented smalti pieces, most famously used in Byzantine mosaics, are set into a matt grey-green background of quartered ceramic tiles. Filled with water, which adds an enhanced jewel-like intensity of colour to the smalti pieces, perhaps your bird bath will attract the curious attention of jays and magpies as well as other smaller garden birds.

Materials

Small dustbin lid, white enamel or galvanized steel

Cement-based adhesive

Bowl

Kitchen knife

Template (see page 126)

Red felt pen

Assortment of smalti in blue, red, orange and green tones – approximately 30 of each colour

Matt ceramic tiles – approximately 130 pale grey-green and 40 darker grey-green

Tile nippers

Face mask and goggles

Rubber gloves

Black grout

Palette knife

Sponge

Soft polishing cloth and/or nail brush

1 If there are any uneven ridges in the upturned lid, even them out by spreading white cement adhesive in the appropriate places. Allow to dry and, using the template, draw eight even, overlapping arcs as shown.

2 Butter the backs of the smalti and, in turn, stick in place a green arc followed by red, followed by orange, then blue. Repeat this pattern around the dustbin lid. Smaller or larger amounts of adhesive will be needed to create an even level as the smalti vary in depth considerably.

3 Wearing the face mask and goggles, cut the paler-coloured ceramic tiles into quarters and fill in the outer areas left between the smalti arcs, nibbling the tiles to fit where necessary with the tile nippers. Continue filling in all segments in the same manner.

4 Cut the darker ceramic tiles into quarters and fill in the central area, following the contours of the arcs and finally filling in the remaining small central section. Gently wipe off any adhesive that has accidentally marked the surface before it dries hard and allow the piece to dry overnight.

5 Mix up some black grout and apply evenly to the surface with a palette knife, pushing the grout well into the gaps. Wear rubber gloves as the black grout can stain.

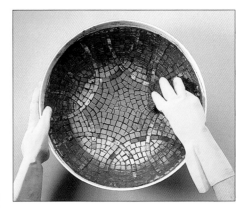

6 After waiting a few minutes, wipe the surface with a barely damp sponge, taking care not to pull any grout out from the gaps whilst removing as much as possible from the surface. Leave to dry, then polish with a cloth or nail brush. The dark grout may have stained the surface of the matt tiles but can be removed with a specialist cleaner (see page 19).

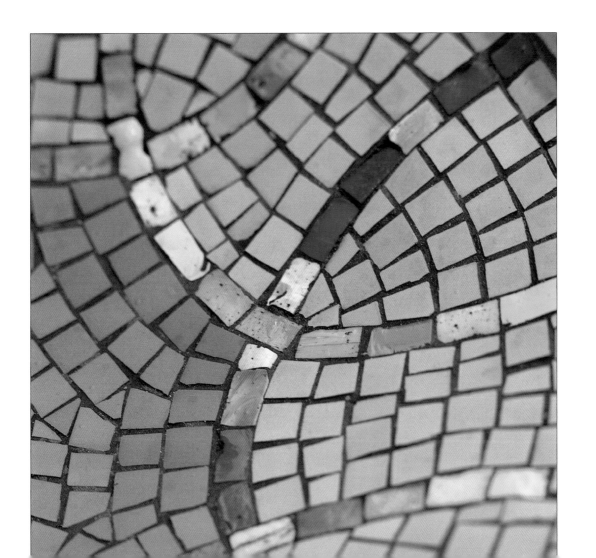

Shell Plant Pot

This simple idea of decorating a flowerpot with a selection of bleached white seashells results in an excellent container for a succulent or cactus plant. It works particularly well if the glaucous or greyish leaves of the plant are chosen carefully to match the serenity of the pale tones of the pot – this design wouldn't suit the bright, somewhat garish tones of a geranium or fuchsia quite so well.

The shells used are not exotic or unusual and it would be quite easy to collect the number used here on a seaside beach. Alternatively, packs of assorted shells are easily available from gift or shell shops in seaside locations. The combination white adhesive tile-and-grout has been used here and any excess has been neatly wiped away with a small paintbrush.

Materials

Tile-and-grout adhesive

32 white cockle shells in 4 sizes

Terracotta pot, approximately 12 cm (4¾ in) high, 15 cm (6 in) in diameter

Pencil

32 pale, flattened spiral shells

8 elongated spirals

Selection of tiny white shells for infilling

Bowl

Kitchen knife

Small paintbrush

1 Use the tile-and-grout adhesive to stick two vertical rows of the cockle shells around the pot. It may help to draw a pencil guideline. Leave about 1.5 cm (⅝ in) gap between the outer edges of the shells and arrange them with the largest overlapping the top of the pot, decreasing in size and placing the smallest at the base.

2 Buttering the backs of the shells, stick the elongated spirals pointing upwards and overlapping at the top of the pot. Continue by sticking four flattened spirals evenly between the cockle shells.

3 Fill in and around the remaining areas of pot with a selection of tiny white shells. It may be easier to dip the end of the shell into the adhesive before sticking in place.

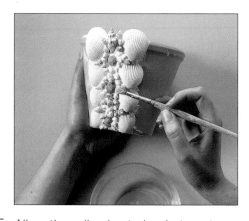

4 Allow the adhesive to begin to set (about 20 minutes), then neaten up the protruding tile-and-grout with a paintbrush dipped in water. Continue sticking shells in this manner around the pot, working and finishing two rows at a time until all is covered.

Pebble Wall Panel

This pebble mosaic is created using the indirect method. This means the design is produced upside down and is only fully revealed when the finished panel is reversed. This is an ideal method for creating panels or slabs to be transported outside, and in particular for making a fairly level surface using irregular elements such as these pebbles. They are all different sizes but, because they are all laid face down onto a flat surface, they appear regular after being set in cement from the back.

This is the perfect project for beachcombers (just remember not to make a habit of collecting too many pebbles) and is a lovely way to display treasured examples that bring back memories of summer holidays. Alternatively, it is now possible to buy quantities of pebbles from home-style shops or garden centres. These black, white and grey-green ones make a very beautiful combination.

Materials

2 lengths of timber
2 x 7 cm (¾ x 2¾ in),
45 cm (18 in) long

2 lengths of timber
2 x 7cm (¾ x 2¾ in),
40 cm (16 in) long

8 screws plus drill and
screwdriver

Piece of plywood 45 cm
(18 in) square

Varnish and brush

Waterproof tape

Bucket of sand

Pencil

Approximately 2 kg
(4½ lb) each of small
black, white and grey-
green pebbles

Small bag of cement

Mixing bowl

Mixing trowel

Piece of expanded metal
or chicken wire

Brush

1 Make the timber up into a frame so the internal measurement is 40 cm (16 in) square and screw together at the corners. Varnish the base and the frame to prevent it warping when in contact with moisture. Place the frame on the plywood base and make a seal with the waterproof tape along the inside edges. Make a level layer of sand in the frame at least 2 cm (¾ in) deep.

2 Using a pencil, draw the border line in the sand 7 cm (2¾ in) in from the sides. Also draw the leaf design within the central section. Begin pushing the grey-green pebbles evenly into the sand on their edges to make a narrow line around the outer edges and along the drawn border.

3 Place four black pebbles equidistantly along each side and fill the space around them with the white pebbles, packing them together as closely as possible.

4 Use the grey-green pebbles to make the leaf stems and one half of the leaves. The three-dimensional effect is created by filling the other half of the leaf design with the white pebbles.

5 Now fill in all around the leaf shapes with the black pebbles, packing them in securely and tightly to fill all the remaining space.

6 Mix the cement three parts sand to one part cement and add just enough water to make it workable (but not too liquid). Mix together thoroughly and pour into the frame to a depth of at least 2.5 cm (1 in). Smooth the surface with a trowel.

7 Cut the expanded metal or chicken wire to fit the square, lay it in the frame and cover with another layer of cement. This layer of cement should be even with the top of the frame.

8 Leave the concrete to set for at least 4 days, then unscrew the frame. Turn the panel upside down very carefully and brush away the unwanted sand. A good blast of water from a hose-pipe jet will clean the panel beautifully.

Tapered Flowerpots

If you have ever attempted to try mosaics before, you have probably ended up making a rather lumpy flowerpot covered in shattered blue-and-white china just like everyone else. But it needn't be like that. These pretty 'long tom' flowerpots have been decorated with a structured design created from antique flower-patterned china and mauve glass tesserae. This unusual combination is set off beautifully with purple-coloured grout.

Never throw away a damaged piece of china, especially if it is a favourite, as it can always be transformed into something else. Including it in the design of a flowerpot means you can enjoy it forever and the work and craftsmanship that went into the original piece are not wasted. It is sensible to use a pot with a lip as this provides a neat way of containing the applied design.

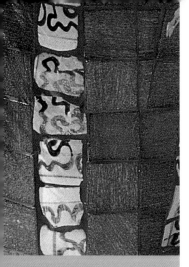

Materials

Tapered flowerpot 15 cm (6 in) high, 12 cm (4¾ in) diameter

Flower-patterned china plates

Tile nippers

Face mask and goggles

Coloured pencil

All-in-one tile and grout adhesive

Small bowl

Kitchen knife

Mauve glass tesserae

White grout powder

Purple acrylic paint

Palette knife

Sponge

Rubber gloves

Craft knife

Soft polishing cloth

1 Use the tile nippers to cut approximately 35 pieces of china 2 cm (¾ in) square, each with a flower motif (wear a face mask and goggles when cutting china). Mark five vertical lines equidistantly around the pot with coloured pencil and stick the china squares in place with the adhesive.

2 Stick the mauve glass tesserae in place alongside the china squares, leaving small gaps between the tiles for the grout. You may need to use more adhesive under the glass tesserae as they will probably be thinner than the china.

3 Lay the next row alongside the second line of china squares and begin cut the tesserae to shape so they fit when the two lines converge. Fill the central gap with shaped pieces, trying to leave an even space for grouting. Continue around the pot, applying the design in this manner until it is completely covered. Remove any adhesive from the surface of the tiles and allow to dry.

4 Add a small quantity of purple paint to some grout powder and mix well with water to make a thick paste. Wearing rubber gloves, apply the grout with the knife, pressing it into the gaps. Leave for 5-10 minutes, then wipe off the excess with a barely damp sponge. Use a knife to remove any unwanted grout from the surface and to make an even edge under the lip of the pot rim. When dry, polish with a clean cloth.

China Shard Saucer

It is surprising how many people build up quite a collection of beautifully patterned china shards. They can often be dug up like treasure in a garden and give fascinating clues to the domestic history of ancestors or simply previous occupants of the house.

This project is the ideal opportunity to incorporate them all into a beautiful and functional object, and at the same time provide an inventive way to display them. A large, flat terracotta saucer has been decorated with the most commonly found shards in many shades of white and the much loved blue-and-white variety.

Some extra cutting and shaping will be necessary to create a neat design. The finished saucer makes an ideal tray on which to place scented candles to enhance an al fresco meal on a summer's evening.

Materials

Chalk

Large terracotta
saucer – this one is
40 cm (16 in) in diameter

Blue-and-white and
white china shards

Tile nippers

Face mask and goggles

Ready-mixed tile
adhesive

Small bowl

Kitchen knife

White powdered grout

Palette knife

Sponge

Soft polishing cloth

1 Using the stick of chalk, draw an even spiral fitting inside the saucer. The spiral here is approximately 3 cm (1¼ in) wide, widening to 4 cm (1½ in) at the mid-section and tapering to a point at each end. If you make a mistake, simply rub out the chalk with your finger and start again.

2 Wearing a face mask and goggles, use the tile nippers to cut the white china to size. Begin laying it glazed side up around the edge of the saucer. Where necessary, cut the shards with the tile nippers to create a smooth curved edge along the chalked spiral. Butter the backs with tile adhesive and stick in position.

3 After you have stuck the shards about halfway round, begin adding the blue china in the same way, starting with the tapered end of the spiral. Continue to work the two colours simultaneously – this enables you to fit the edges of the two colours together neatly.

4 Continue until the saucer is completed, making sure that no adhesive protrudes through the gaps. Mix the grout in a bowl following the packet instructions and spread across the surface with the palette knife, pushing it firmly into the spaces. Leave to dry for 30 minutes, then wipe off the excess with a damp sponge. Leave for another 30 minutes, then polish with a soft cloth.

Pebble and Terracotta Paving Slab

This striking terrace design has been made by assembling eight paving

slabs decorated with crisp white pebbles and pieces of broken terracotta

flowerpots. The design has been inspired by simple patchwork quilt

patterns and, in the same way that quilts are usually made from a collection

of old pieces of fabric, these paving slabs are created using found pebbles

and shards of discarded garden pots.

This simple project employs the indirect method

of making mosaics where the design is created upside

down in a frame which is then filled with cement.

After a few days the frame is removed and the slab is

turned the right way up to reveal the finished design.

Materials

Casting frame, internal measurement 30 cm (12 in) square

1 small cup soft sand

Pencil

Tile nippers

Broken terracotta pots

Face mask and goggles

Small white pebbles

Bag of mixed sand and cement – 4 kg (9 lb) for each slab – or mix your own, three parts sand to one part cement

Bowl or bucket for mixing cement

Cement trowel

Piece of chicken wire 30 cm (12 in) square

Screwdriver

Steel brush

1 Empty the sand into the base of the casting frame and spread evenly over the surface. Draw your design into the sand with a pencil, dividing the area into four equal sections. Draw a smaller square in the centre of each larger square.

2 Wearing a face mask and goggles, use the tile nippers to cut the pots into squares and rectangles and begin to fill in the previously drawn design. Fill the diagonally opposite large squares leaving the smaller centres free. On the remaining opposite squares, fill in the middle smaller sections as shown.

3 Now fill in the remaining areas with the contrasting white pebbles. Place them close together, making sure that they sit securely in the thin layer of sand. Place the flattest side down for an even finished surface.

4 Add water to the cement mix to make a slightly wet mixture. Lay trowelfuls carefully on top of the design and tamp it down with the edge of the trowel to encourage the mixture to cover all around the pebbles and terracotta pieces. Take great care when doing this to avoid dislodging any of the elements.

5 After the frame has been half filled with the cement mixture, lay the piece of chicken wire on top and continue to fill with the cement until level with the frame. Smooth the top over and put aside to dry.

6 Cement takes a number of days to cure completely but the frame edges may be removed after a couple of days to assist the drying. After another two days the slab may be turned over carefully and the sand can be hosed off, revealing the finished design. Any unwanted cement that has squeezed too far through the pebbles can be removed with a steel brush.

Garden Flowers

These eye-catching mosaic flowers on metal stems are just the thing to brighten your garden during the dull days of winter when little else is flowering. Alternatively, if pushed into a brightly coloured summer flowerbed, their glittering petals will compete with and complement the most exotic blooms.

The flowers are made from a collection of plain-coloured, patterned and lustre china stuck onto a metal background and grouted in black to make the different colours sing out. If you prefer, you could fix them directly to a garden wall and add mosaic stems and leaves. Once you have mastered this particular project you may like to branch out and make bees, butterflies, birds, frogs, snails or other decorative garden inhabitants.

Materials

Template (see page 126)

Tin or aluminium sheet 0.5 mm (1⁄32 in) thick, 20 cm (8 in) square for each flower

Felt pen

Strong scissors or tin snips

Coarse sandpaper

Quick-setting resin adhesive

Flattened galvanized steel or aluminium strip 3 mm (1⁄8 in) thick, 9 mm (3⁄8 in) wide and 50 cm (20 in) long

Selection of china, such as yellow, blue, black-and-white patterned, gold lustre

Tile nippers

Face mask and goggles

Cement-based adhesive

Bowl

Kitchen knife

Orange and gold glass tesserae

Black grout

Rubber gloves

Sponge

Nail brush

Soft polishing cloth

1 Lay the template on the piece of metal and draw around with a felt pen and cut out with scissors or tin snips. Roughly sand both sides of the metal with the course sandpaper to provide a key for the resin adhesive. Mix up the adhesive as on the packet instructions and use a generous quantity to stick the stem in place in the middle of the back of the flower shape.

2 Wearing a face mask and goggles, cut eight small triangular petal shapes (see page 17), butter the backs with adhesive and stick in place on the front of the metal flower.

3 Cut the glass tesserae into quarters and make a ring of alternate orange and gold pieces just inside the petals. Take care not to use too much adhesive – it should not squeeze up between the individual pieces.

4 Using the patterned and gold lustre pieces, make a random jigsaw pattern in the centre of the flower. Use the tile nippers to cut the china to fit.

5 Use the tile nippers to cut small pieces of dark blue china to make a rim around the yellow triangular petals. Always remember to adjust the amount of adhesive on the back of each piece in order to create an even and level finished surface. Leave to dry overnight.

6 Mix up some black grout. Wearing the rubber gloves, cover the flower with grout, working it into the crevices with a small knife. Also grout around the edges of the petals for a neat finish. Leave for a few minutes and rub off excess with a barely damp sponge. If the surface is uneven, leave for longer and remove with a nail brush. When dry, polish with a cloth.

Shell Wall Motifs

Shell-encrusted grottoes were very fashionable in the eighteenth century and consequently became an essential feature in a newly planned garden. The exuberant decoration using all manner of shells in a purpose-built summer house, bath house or gazebo can only be marvelled at. Creating a shell grotto is an adventurous, not to say expensive project and so these simple little shell rosettes are an ideal introduction to working in an inspiring medium.

Collect your shell varieties from the beach, but for environmental reasons, don't take too many. Restaurants are another good source for lovely patterned clams and iridescent mussels to take home in a doggy bag! Some general gift shops, particularly at the seaside, sell inexpensive packs of assorted shells ideal for this project.

Materials

Felt pen

White ceramic tile 10 cm
(4 in) square

Tile nippers

Face mask and goggles

Circular compact mirror
approximately 6 cm
(2½ in) in diameter

Tile-and-grout adhesive

Bowl

Kitchen knife

Assorted shells including
16 spiral shapes,
8 cockle-type halves
and a flatter spiral for
the centre

Small paintbrush

Cottonbud

1 Using felt pen, draw a circle onto the ceramic tile. Wearing a face mask and goggles, use the tile nippers to nibble away the edges along this guideline to make the circular shape.

2 Put a quantity of adhesive onto the back of the mirror and stick in place on the underside of the tile – as this is the unglazed side there will be better adhesion.

3 Butter the flatter, open edge of the spiral shells and stick them all around the mirror in a tight circle. The adhesive should make contact with both the tile and the edge of the mirror and should be sufficient to hold the shell in place without messily squeezing out from underneath when pushed into place.

4 Cover up the edges of the spiral shells with the broad sides of the cockle variety. You will need to apply more adhesive at the contact point between the shells to fit them neatly and securely.

5 Butter the back of the central shell with adhesive and push into place in the centre of the remaining mirror.

6 Allow the adhesive about 15 minutes to begin setting, then neaten and remove all the excess adhesive with a slightly damp paintbrush. If necessary, the exposed mirror can be cleaned with a cottonbud.

Garden Shelf

This elegant individual shelf provides the ideal place for exhibiting a favourite plant in the garden so that it stands well apart from all others.

Small town gardens are often surrounded by high brick walls, so use must be made of all the available space to its best advantage. It is now very popular to paint these walls with a limewash coloured with natural pigments which, if chosen carefully, can make a stunning background for growing plants, hanging pots or, as in this case, for fixing the pretty mosaiced shelf to.

The little wooden shelf was bought in kit form in a home-style shop. However, it did need to be varnished well to prevent the wood from swelling when it gets wet out in the garden. The restrained design has been created by covering the assembled shelf with white china dotted with flower motifs whilst selected flower-patterned china has been carefully cut to fit around the edges.

Materials

Shelf kit, approximately 16 x 19 cm (6½ x 7½ in)

Exterior varnish and brush

Broken white china

Tile nippers

Face mask and goggles

Tile-and-grout adhesive

Bowl

Small knife

27 rosebud motifs cut from china

Flower-patterned china for edges

Palette knife

Sponge

Soft polishing cloth

1 Assemble and varnish the shelf. Allow to dry. Wearing a face mask and goggles, use the tile nippers to cut the china to size. Stick the broken white china on the underside of the shelf as shown in a crazy paving pattern, buttering the back of each piece and cutting as necessary to make a neat fit against the next.

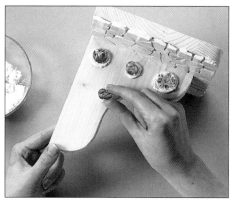

2 On each side of the shelf support, stick seven rosebud motifs equally spaced. When using china of differing thicknesses, adjust the amount of adhesive used to make the finished surface level.

3 Cut and fit more white china around these rosebuds and make sure that the edges of the china are cut flush with the edge of the wood. Repeat on the other side.

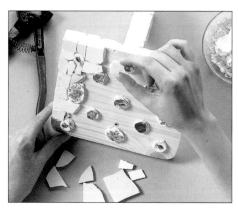

4 Employing the same technique, stick 13 rosebud motifs on the top surface of the shelf and surround them with carefully cut pieces of white china.

5 Leave the shelf to set for a couple of hours so the pieces will not be dislodged when adding the edges. Use the tile nippers to cut the flower-patterned china into pieces that cover the shelf support. Butter the backs with adhesive and stick them neatly all along the edge of the shelf support.

6 Cut similar pieces for the front and side edges of the shelf and stick in place, leaving small gaps between them. Allow to set, then grout and polish (see page 19).

Templates

Butterfly Tiles (page 34)

Oak Leaf Table (page 22)
Enlarge on a photocopier to 200%

Cup-and-Saucer Tray (page 40)

Bird Bath (page 86)
Enlarge on a photocopier to 142% (A4 to A3)

Garden Flowers (page 112)
Enlarge on a photocopier
to 142% (A4 to A3)

Victorian Boots (page 54)
Enlarge on a photocopier to 142% (A4 to A3)

Suppliers

UK

Edgar Udney & Co Ltd
314 Balham High Street
London SW17 7AA
Tel: 0171 767 8181
Suppliers of ceramic and glass tesserae and smalti, as well as adhesives and grout. Mail order available.

The Mosaic Workshop
Unit B
443-449 Holloway Road
London N7 6LJ
Tel: 0171 263 2997
Suppliers of glass, ceramic, marble and stone tesserae, adhesives, tools, grout, backing boards and all associated mosaic materials. Mail order available. Also runs mosaic courses.

Tower Ceramics Ltd
91 Parkway
London NW1 9PP
Tel: 0171 485 7192
Suppliers of ceramic tiles, marble and terracotta, adhesives, grout, cleaning materials and mosaic tools.

Fred Aldous
PO Box 135
37 Lever Street
Manchester 1 M60 1UX
Tel: 0161 236 2477 (general enquiries),
0161 236 4224 (mail order)
Mail order supplier of mosaic tools and materials.

Specialist Crafts Ltd
P O Box 247
Leicester LE1 9QS
Tel: 0116 253 3139
Mail order supplier of mosaic tools and materials.

Mosaic Matters
Web site: http://www.asm.dircon.co.uk
This 'online magazine for all things mosaic' offers feature articles about mosaics, exhibitions, how-to tips, listings of workshops and a Q&A section.

USA

Art Source
PO Box 4104
Clifton Park, NY 12605
Toll free: (800) 405-6363
Fax: (518) 371-9423
Web site: http://www.artglasssource.com
Mosaic tiles, glass, grout, stepping stone molds, glass cutters, lamp kits, mosaic table bases and more. Call for a complete catalog.

Mountaintop Mosaic
PO Box 653
Castleton, VT 05735-0653
Toll free: (800) 564-4980
Fax: (802) 468-2183
Web site: http://www.mountaintopmosaics.com
Supplier of vitreous glass, smalti, mosaic tiles and tools.

Stroke of Genius
2326 Fillmore Street
San Francisco, CA 94115
Tel: (415 776-2529
Fax: (415) 776-2543
Carries vitreous glass tesserae, cut stained glass, glass gems, broken ceramic tiles, tools, adhesive, grout and accessories. Call for a complete catalog.

Mendel's
1556 Haight Street
San Francisco, CA 94117
Tel: (415) 621-1287
Fax: (415) 621-6587
Web site: http://www.mendels.com
Art and craft supply store with a large selection of mosaic glass, tiles and tools.

Fleetwood Building Block
240 W. Main Street
Fleetwood, PA 19522
Tel: (610) 944-8385
Fax: (610) 944-0827
Web site: http://www.fleetwoodblock.com/fieldbed2.htm
Sells 50 lb bags of 1-3″ pebbles in plum, emerald, roseate and black.

Timber merchants: A good timber merchant will cut wood and board to your exact measurements for a little extra cost.

Tile shops: Most tile shops sell a wide variety of ceramic materials, tools, adhesives and grout. Occasionally they may be prepared to give you broken tiles.

Charity shops, flea markets and jumble sales: All good sources for finding cheap, coloured or patterned china.

Hardware shops: Supply nails, screws, resin, adhesives and tools.

Builders merchants or architectural ironmongers: Usually supply sheet metal, aluminium, brass or copper.

Blanks for decorating: Stores such as Habitat or IKEA are good sources of plain items such as trays and shelves ideal for decorating with mosaics.

Index

Page numbers in **bold** type refer to projects. Page numbers in *italic* type refer to illustrations.